The Divine Liturgy

A Simple Guide For The Common Person

PRESVYTERA ELEFTHERIA RECACHINAS

The Divine Liturgy

A Simple Guide For The Common Person

PUBLISHED BY
PRESVYTERA ELEFTHERIA RECACHINAS
CONNECTICUT, USA

Published October 2010
by Presv. Eleftheria Recachinas

Printed and bound in the
United States of America

ISBN-13: 978-0-9829744-0-7

The Divine Liturgy – A Simple Guide for the Common Person

Cover & Book Design by Vicky Spyrou-Andriotis
Prepared for Publication by Vicky Spyrou-Andriotis

To Tasso, Katerina, and Emmanuel, the joy and light of my life!

Contents

Preface

The main reason for writing this book is the need I see around me- the need to know what is going on during the Divine Liturgy. For many years I have observed and noticed that some of the faithful do not know when they should sit or stand. They do not know when it is the appropriate time to enter the Church or to move around. The reason for this is that they don't really know what it is that's taking place in front of them. This doesn't mean that they are indifferent or that their mind wanders. The reason simply is that they don't know. No matter how many times a Priest or someone else explains the Liturgy or its parts, common questions still remain of how someone should behave during the Divine Liturgy.

There is a plethora of books written by great theologians, Priests and Bishops explaining the Divine Liturgy. I am not a theologian, nor do I pretend to be. What I try to accomplish here is to explain, in simple words, what I was taught by my parents; my extended family; my Sunday school, high school and college professors; and from my knowledge acquired through reading books. This book comes from my heart, intended so anyone who wants to know, young or old, can understand and benefit from it.

There are so many people that I personally want to thank. First, my parents: my father, a theologian and teacher by profession, an orator by virtue, who was appointed by the Metropolitan to preach the Gospel every Sunday throughout my native island of Rhodes; my mother, a simple, soft, and saintly woman with an unshakeable faith. Both, filled with deep faith in God, taught me and molded me into who I am and what I know.

Secondly, my husband: a very dedicated, patient, committed, selfless, hard working Priest for his support and encouragement. After thirty-three years, he still inspires me with his love and devotion to his ministry.

To Tasso, Katerina and Emmanuel, our children, for offering their comments and opinions.

To Shauna Maher, a magazine writer, for her time reading my manuscript and making suggestions from a non-Orthodox reader's point-of-view.

I offer my gratitude to Ioanna Pettas Opidee, author and professor at Fairfield University, whose immense writing skills helped me with editing this book.

To Vicky Andriotis, an author and most multitalented person I've ever met. As an experienced and knowledgeable author, she guided and helped me publish this book.

Vicky, I deeply appreciate you for sharing your expertise with me, and thank you for your patience, understanding, and guidance.

The Ladies of Philoptochos Society of Holy Trinity Connecticut for allowing me to publish their recipes.

Last but not least, I thank the faithful of Holy Trinity Bridgeport, Connecticut, whose thirst for knowledge inspired me to write this book.

Introduction

In the Orthodox Church today, we mainly celebrate three Divine Liturgies. They are: The Liturgy of St. Basil the Great, the Liturgy of St. John the Chrysostom, and the Liturgy of the Pre-Sanctified Gifts. We also have other Liturgies that we do not usually celebrate except on specific days, such as the Saint's Name day. The first and oldest is the Liturgy of St. James (Iakovos), first Bishop of Jerusalem, whose feast day is celebrated on October 23rd. The second is the Liturgy of St. Mark, founder of the Church of Alexandria, who is celebrated on April 25th; and the third is the Liturgy of St. Gregory the Theologian, whose feast day is on January 25th .

The Liturgy of St. Basil the Great is a longer service with additional hymns and prayers which is celebrated ten times a year: on his feast day January 1st; on the first five Sundays of the Great Lent; on Holy Thursday morning; on Holy Saturday morning; on Christmas; and on the Epiphany of our Lord, on January 6th. The Liturgy of St. Chrysostom is celebrated every Sunday and every feast day, with the exception of those mentioned above. Finally, we have the Liturgy of the Pre-Sanctified Gifts, which is celebrated on Wednesdays and Fridays during the Great Lent. It is called Pre-Sanctified because the gifts, which we will discuss later on, are already blessed and sanctified from the previous Sunday.

The Divine Liturgy is the work of all people, and it is conducted for our benefit. The Priest cannot conduct the Divine Liturgy alone; at least one person must be present. The people -- members of the faithful community who wish to do so -- offer the gifts: the *Prosphor*o (bread) and the wine. They, as one body, together with the Priest, make up the Church. As we hear in the hymn to St. Spyridon during the Liturgy, all the Angels -- Seraphim and Cherubim -- are present, co-celebrating with the Priest. Imagine and feel, their presence, as you get ready to be uplifted spiritually.

The parts of the Divine Liturgy correspond with the different periods in Christ's life, and each part has its own symbolism. In essence, it is as Christ's life is unfolding before our very own eyes. It is up to us to see and accept this and welcome Him in.

Beforehand, during the Orthros or Matins service, the Priest conducts the *Proskomidi*, or the Offeratory. He prepares the bread and wine that, will later- during the Sanctification- be transformed into the body and blood of Christ. We, the faithful, do not see how the Priest prepares the gifts, which represents the mystery of the unknown years of Christ's early life on earth.

Theologians tell us of different parts of the Divine Liturgy. To make it simple and easier to understand, I will divide it into two parts: the Preparation, which ends after the Creed is recited, and the Sacramental. The Preparation corresponds to Christ's life from the time He started His ministry, teaching, healing and performing miracles. The Sacramental corresponds to His Sacrifice on the Cross, His death and His Resurrection.

It is very important that we are present from the beginning of the service. The Divine Liturgy is conducted for our benefit, and each part is significant. Christ's Grace comes upon us by hearing His Word, sharing in His Sacrifice, rejoicing in His Resurrection and accepting Him as our God and Savior through Holy Communion.

In this book, I will try to explain – in simple, rather than theological terms -- the Divine Liturgy. I will provide information on fasting and preparing for Holy Communion and on Memorials, as well as the guidelines of the Greek Orthodox Archdiocese on these and other matters. I have also included recipes for *Prosphoro, Kolyva, and Artoklasia.* I pray that you will find something that will touch you -- something you will use and incorporate into your spiritual life as you attend the liturgical service.

Chapter One

THE PARTS OF THE CHURCH

Before we discuss the Divine Liturgy in more depth, I will briefly explain the three parts of the Church, also known as the *Naos* or *Ekklisia.* They are the Narthex, the Nave and the Sanctuary, which represent the Earth, Sky and Heavens, respectively, according to St. Symeon.

THE NARTHEX

The Narthex is where we enter the Church. In the early years of the Church, the catechumens (those who were taught the faith but weren't yet Christians, and therefore could not receive Holy Communion) stood in the Narthex during the Divine Liturgy.

The Narthex is the place of "preparation" where we light our candles and venerate the icons in order to prepare ourselves spiritually before we enter the Nave. Here, we find two candle stands, which symbolize a tomb. According to our faith, before Christ's birth, and as a result of our disobedience in Paradise, we humans were spiritually dead. The candles we take as we enter the Church signify our dead self. By lighting and placing them in the symbolic tomb, we become spiritually resurrected.

It is suggested that we light at least one candle on each side -- one for the health of our living loved ones, and one for the soul of those who are dead -- while praying for the people for whom we light them. However, each of us may determine the number we wish to light; many people light one for every member of their family.

After lighting our candles, we move on to venerate the icons, which are placed in the *Proskinitari* (Icon stand). To do this, we cross ourselves by joining together the thumb, the index and the middle finger of the right hand, while bending the other two fingers to touch the palm. The three joined fingers symbolize the One God in the three Persons of the Holy Trinity (Father, Son and Holy Spirit), while the other two symbolize the two natures of Christ: the Human and the Divine. We then kiss the feet or the body of the saint who is depicted on the icon. Out of reverence and humility, we should not kiss the face.

Some, especially older women, are seen making prostrations (bending over in prayer) in front of icons, thus expressing their faith and spirituality. Spirituality is an essential part of our worship. It enables us to see and feel things differently, but unfortunately it can be missing in our practices today.

Conversations should be avoided in the Narthex so as not disrupt the attention of the people within the Nave, which is where the faithful stand or sit in the pews while attending services.

THE NAVE

The Nave is the largest and most ornate part of the Church. The walls are adorned with icons depicting the life of Christ from His Birth to His Resurrection and Ascension, as well as icons of Saints.

Most Orthodox Churches have a dome on the ceiling, which displays the icon of Christ *Pantokrator*, the one who holds the whole world. On the four corners of the dome are icons depicting the images of the four Evangelists: John, Mathew, Mark, and Luke. The dome represents the Heavens, while the floor of the Nave represents the Earth.

The next part of the Church is the Sanctuary, or Holy Altar. The area in front of the Sanctuary, which is usually elevated by a step or two, is called the *solea.* The Bishop's Throne, the *Despotikon*, is on the right side of the *solea*, bearing the icon of Christ the Archpriest. Thus, only the Bishop, who is the Archpriest, is allowed on the the throne. The pulpit is on the left side of the solea and is used by the Deacon or the Priest for the reading of the Gospel or for the Sermon. The *Analogion*, which holds the books used by the cantors and readers during the Divine Liturgy, is next to the Bishop's throne.

The *Iconostasis* -- a tall screen adorned with icons and containing three doors -- divides the Sanctuary from both the *solea* and the Nave, thereby separating the earthly from the divine. The center and largest door of the Iconostasis is called the Great Door, also known as the Beautiful or Royal Door. Only the Priest and the Bishop can enter the altar through this door and only during services. After services the door is kept closed. In the old times, the doorway was closed by a screen depicting Christ. Today, it is closed by a velvet curtain.

The icons on the *Iconostasis* follow the same order in each and every Greek Orthodox Church. The door on the far right displays the icon of Archangel Gabriel, while the one on the far left shows the icon of Archangel Michael. These are the guardians of the Holy Altar. To the immediate right of the Great Door is the icon of Christ, with the icon of St. John the Baptist next to Him. To the immediate left of the Royal Door is the icon of Theotokos. Next to Her is the icon of the saint to whom the Church is dedicated. For example, if you see the icon of the Holy Trinity, you know that that particular Church is dedicated to the Holy Trinity. If you see the icon of St. George, that Church is called St. George's Church.

THE HOLY ALTAR

During the Consecration of each Greek Orthodox Church, the Bishop places relics of saints and martyrs in the altar hidden inside the Holy Table. The Holy Table, also known as Altar Table, is placed in the center of the Sanctuary. The table is called Holy because it is where the mystery of the Holy Eucharist takes place.

The following articles are found on the Holy Table:

The Holy Gospel - a large, gold or silver, richly-decorated book that contains the four gospels. One side depicts the Crucifixion of Christ, and the other the Resurrection. At the four corners are the four Evangelists: John Mathew, Mark and Luke.

The Cross- which is made of gold or silver mid-sized metal and is richly-ornate with semiprecious stones, is used by the Priest or Bishop to bless the faithful.

The *Ieratikon*- a book used by the Priest, that contains all the Liturgies, Vespers, Matins, and all the services that are conducted in the Church.

The *Artophorion* or Tabernacle- an ornate vessel shaped like a Church, in which Holy Communion is kept throughout the year for emergencies and for the sick.

The Eternal Light- a votive light placed directly in front of the *Artophorion* that burns constantly.

The *Antiminsion*- a cloth that depicts the burial of Christ, with relics of saints sewed in one corner. It is kept folded under the Holy Gospel until after the Cherubic Hymn, when it is unfolded and placed in the center of the Altar Table. On it, the Priest will place the gifts that will be transformed and consecrated. A liturgy cannot be performed without this Cloth, in or outside the Church. It is signed by the presiding Bishop, thus giving permission to the Priest to conduct the Divine Liturgy.

The *Exapteriga*- consists of three metal objects: one large Cross and two round large disks. They are made of gold or silver and are placed at the back of the Holy Table. The disks depict the six-winged Seraphim who, along with the Cherubim, are present at every Divine Liturgy. Prophet Isaiah describes the Seraphim as (6:2) "each with six wings; with two they covered their faces, with two they covered their feet, and with two they were flying." The Cross, which bears the Crucifixion on one side and the Resurrection on the other, is placed in the middle. They are used during the Great Entrance of every Divine Liturgy and during other religious processions.

The Crucifix- a large wooden Cross where the life-sized body of Christ is nailed. This is placed directly behind the metal Cross as a constant reminder of His sacrifice for our salvation. It is used every Holy Thursday evening. As we all know, on Holy Thursday evening we commemorate the Passion and Crucifixion of our Lord. After the fifth

Gospel reading, the Priest carries the Cross out of the Altar in a procession and places it in the middle of the *solea* in remembrance of Jesus carrying His Cross to Golgotha.

The Altar walls are filled with life-sized icons of the three Hierarchs or of the great Fathers of the Church. On the ceiling behind the Altar Table is a larger icon called ***Platytera***, which depicts the Theotokos holding Christ. This symbolizes the unity of Earth and Heaven, the earthly with the divine, since through Her (*Panagia*), Christ came to save the human race, and through His Passion and Resurrection, we are able to achieve life everlasting.

On the left wall is the ***Prothesis***, which is where the Priest prepares the gifts. The preparation takes place during the Matins; therefore, it is recommended that the people offering the gifts bring them to the Church early in the morning or the day before. The *Prothesis*, which is a concave inlet in the wall of the altar, symbolizes the stable of Bethlehem where Christ was born. The vessels used for the preparation are:

The *Diskarion* (also Disk or Paten)- which symbolizes the manger. It is a round metal disk on a pedestal where the "*Amnos*" or the "Lamb of God"-- the center of the seal on the *Prosphoron* -- is placed with many more smaller pieces representing the Theotokos, the Angels, the Prophets, the Apostles, the Holy Fathers, other Saints and the people that offered the gifts.

The Chalice- a gold or silver, large-stemmed drinking cup, where the wine is placed. It symbolizes the cup which Christ drank for our salvation.

The Lance- a spear-shaped knife with a double edge at the top, which the Priest uses to cut the *Amnos* (the Host) and other portions from the *Prosphoron.* It symbolizes the spear that pierced Christ's side while He was on the Cross.

The Lavida- or the spoon with which the Holy Communion is administered. Our sins are cleansed as we partake of the Holy Communion with this spoon, just as the Seraphim cleansed Isaiah from his sins, using tongs to touch his lips with a hot coal taken from the Altar (Isaiah-6:7).

The Sponge- used to remove any drop of Holy Communion that is left in the

Holy Chalice, which the Priest must consume. This symbolizes the sponge the soldiers dipped in vinegar and water and gave to Jesus nailed on the Cross.

The Asterisk- a metal object in the shape of the cross, which is placed on top of the *Diskarion*, and symbolizes the star of Bethlehem.

The Three Covers- one for the Disk, one for the Chalice and a larger one that the Priest places over his shoulders during the Great Entrance. They symbolize the shroud of Christ. After the Priest places the Holy Gifts on the Altar Table, he covers both with the larger cloth, to represent the burial of Christ and the rolling of the stone that closed Christ's tomb. During the Creed, the Priest gently shakes the larger cloth over the gifts in remembrance of the earthquake that rolled the big stone and opened the tomb of Christ.

The Zeon- a small, pitcher-like vessel that is filled with warm water that the Priest uses for Holy Communion. This water represents the warm water and blood that flowed out of Jesus' side when it was pierced while on the Cross. It also symbolizes the warm faith that should draw us to the Holy Cup.

The Censer or *Thimiaton*- a cup hanging from three chains decorated with twelve bells. The chains symbolize The Father, Son, and Holy Spirit, the three persons of Holy Trinity. The bells represent the twelve Apostles. The cup stands for the Theotokos, the vehicle through whom Christ became man, and the incense that burns within and emerges from it signifies our prayers.

The *Prosphoron*- a round loaf of bread without which a liturgy cannot be performed. It is an offering from the faithful to Christ Himself. The round shape symbolizes the infinite Christ. From the seal on the prosphoron, the Priest, using the lance, will cut the following pieces: first the *Amnos*, bearing the letters IC XP NI KA, which mean "Jesus Christ Conquers." These letters were seen in the sky in a vision by Constantine, the Emperor of Constantinople, before an important victorious battle. This is the piece (*Amnos*) which will be transformed into the Body of Christ. Additional pieces are cut from the seal for the Theotokos, the

Archangels and Angels, the Prophets, the Apostles, the Holy Fathers, the Martyrs, the Holy Ascetics, the Holy Unmercenaries, the parents of Panagia, Joachim and Anna, all the Saints including those whose memory and liturgy are celebrated that day, the Archbishop, the Priests, the Deacons, the Bishops, all the people who offered the gifts that day, the fathers of the Church, those whose names are commemorated that day, the name of the saint the Church is named after; and, at the end, a piece for the Priest himself.

Finally, **the Wine or *Nama*,** which is red, and symbolizes the blood of Christ.

Chapter Two

THE CLERGY

Clergymen in the Orthodox Church are allowed to marry only before their ordination. Once they are ordained, they are considered descendants of Christ. Christ, the High Priest, conferred His Priesthood to His Apostles and, from them, to all the clergy through the Apostolic Succession by the hand of the ordaining Bishop.

The ranks of clergy are:

The Deacon- whose main responsibility is to assist the Priest or the Bishop during the services. The Deacon cannot celebrate the Divine Liturgy, perform sacraments, or administer the Holy Communion by himself (except in extreme emergencies). A Deacon can become a Priest through the Ordination to Priesthood if he has completed his required theological education.

The Priest- can conduct all services and sacraments, except the Sacrament of Holy Ordination. The Priest is the central of all ranks. Only a Priest can celebrate the Divine Liturgy by himself. A Bishop cannot, unless he dresses as a Priest or co-celebrates with a Priest.

The Bishop- the highest title that a celibate Priest can achieve. In order to become a Bishop one has to go through the two previous ranks. Every diocese or metropolis has a Bishop. A Bishop can also receive honors: he can be a titular Bishop, which is an assistant to another Bishop; a Metropolitan, which is head of metropolis or diocese; Archbishop; and, the highest of all, Patriarch.

A married Priest cannot become a Bishop, but he can receive other honorary titles called *offikia,* such as ***Economos, Pnevmatikos*** (Father Confessor) among others, and the highest of these honors, *Protopresvyteros* (Protopresbyter). As Protopresbyter he can wear a special, decorated Cross on a long chain. A celibate Priest also receives the title of *Archimandrite* and can become Bishop through Ordination.

Ordinations may take place during any Divine Liturgy, and can only be conducted by a Bishop. A Bishop can ordain Deacons and Priests by himself but can only ordain Bishops with the assistance of at least one other Bishop.

PREPARATION FOR THE DIVINE LITURGY

Before the Priest begins the *Orthros*, or Matins, and then the Divine Liturgy, he takes the time, or *Kairos*, to prepare. In his black robe, he stands in the middle of the *solea* and faces the door of the Holy Altar, which is presently closed. He reads special prayers, and venerates the icons of Christ first, then of Theotokos, then those of St. John the Baptist, the saint the Church is dedicated to, and the icons of the Archangels on the two side doors. Throughout all this, he prays and asks God to enable him to enter His Holy Altar clean from every sin, unblemished, and worthy to prepare the sacrament of the Holy Eucharist. He is the vehicle through whom, by the Divine Grace, the gifts will be transformed into the **Sacred Body and Blood** of Christ for our salvation. Because he offers and holds the **Holiest of Gifts** in his hands, it is customary to kiss the right hand of the Priest when we greet him. The practice of kissing the Priest's hand is slowly disappearing. Some think of the Priest as their friend; others do not know of the reason that we should kiss his hand.

Here is where spirituality can help us understand. We should not forget the role a Priest plays in bringing us closer to the Holy Cup and through It to our salvation. His hands are holding the Holiest of Holy. By kissing his hand, we not only show our respect and thankfulness towards the person through whom Holy Communion is administered to us, but also our humble, selfless existence towards God.

This preparation enables the Priest to be transformed spiritually and mentally from the earthly to the divine. He enters the Sanctuary, makes three prostrations in front of the Holy Altar, and kisses the Holy Gospel and the Holy Table. At this point, he is prepared to begin the service.

VESTMENTS OF THE PRIEST

Before the Priest begins the Divine Liturgy, he vests himself while he recites a special prayer for each item of his vestments as he puts it on:

The *Sticharion,* or Alb- which extends to his feet and is usually a solid color, without much decoration. It symbolizes the robe the Jews put on Jesus before the crucifixion.

The *Epitrachelion*, or Stole- a long, narrow, decorated cloth that goes over the Priest's neck and reaches just above the hem of the *Stiharion.* The Priest cannot perform any service without the *Epitrachelion.* It signifies the Grace of the Holy Spirit that comes upon him.

The *Zoni*, or Belt- which he places around his waist. It helps with his movements and signifies the Divine Strength he receives from above.

The *Epimanica,* or Cuffs- which he fastens around his wrists in order to facilitate his movements and which signify the chains that were put around the hands of Jesus.

The *Epigonation-* a decorated piece that is hung from the Zoni and it is worn by Priests that were granted a special honor -- *officio* -- by their Bishop . It looks like a sword, signifying the power of the Holy Spirit.

The *Felonion,* or Chasuble- is largest of the layers and is worn on top of the rest. A decorated Cross is sewn on the back, so the Priest who wears it is symbolically carrying his Cross, as Christ carried His own Cross. The *Felonion* also symbolizes the robe Jesus wore in front of Pilate and the robes that the Apostles wore during their travels.

The Cross- As mentioned above, only the Priests that were given the high honor of *Protopresbyter* by their Bishop can wear the Cross over their vestments.

After the Priest vests himself, he washes his hands and prays that he will be cleansed from his sins. Enlightened by all this preparation, the Priest approaches the *Prothesis* to prepare the gifts, as described above.

As we see, the Priest doesn't walk right into the Church and start the liturgy. There is an extensive physical, mental, spiritual and emotional preparation that takes place. Similarly, we need to prepare ourselves if we want to benefit from what it is taking place in front of us. We must prepare through spiritual exercise in order to benefit form the Grace of God.

Usually, young mothers prepare the Sunday clothes of their children on Saturday afternoon or evening. Likewise, all of us should prepare ourselves through prayer and meditation.

It can be difficult to pray. Our everyday tasks and family concerns consume our whole life. It is up to us to not allow them to become an overwhelming burden. We must set aside time for prayer or for reading the Bible. But, just as when the doctor prescribes certain exercise for any aching pain, we do not heal right away; it takes time and continuous exercise for the healing to set in. We must be persistent in setting time for prayer. Through practice, it gets easier to pray.

Distractions are everywhere. Even during services, we are easily distracted. We go to Church to pray and to receive God's Grace. We should be sensitive to the needs of everyone and be careful not to disturb or disrupt others with our behavior.

There are certain times during the Divine Liturgy when we should not enter the Nave or move around. They are:

- **During the Great Doxology**
- **At the beginning of the Divine Liturgy,** when the Priest says "Blessed is the Kingdom of the Father, Son and Holy Spirit"
- **Every time the Priest faces the faithful**
- **While the Priest is reading the Gospel**

- **Every time the Priest is in the *solea***. As we will describe later, he is there during the Small and Great Entrances, Memorials or *Artoklasia* services, and other processions.

- **While we recite the Creed and the Sunday Prayer** ("Our Father", or "*Pater Imon*")

- **During the Sanctification of the Holy Gifts** which is the most sacred moment of the Divine Liturgy.

We should attend the Divine Liturgy often, if not every Sunday. The reasons for this are, as St. Maximos writes, because the angels make note of all present and they pray to God for them, and also because, with our presence, we can be transformed through the Divine Grace. According to St. John the Chrysostom, when we come out of Church, we are transformed: our faces appear as if we came down for Heaven. If we come in sad, we leave happy; if we come in angry or troubled we leave in peace. This is because of His Grace.

As mentioned earlier, the Priest prepares himself before every Divine Liturgy. It is rather important that we do the same. Before we enter the Church we should leave our worldly concerns behind and commit ourselves to what we are about to witness.

Remember to turn off your cell phones or other devices that might disturb others. Discard your gum or candy, or save them for later. It is very disrespectful to chew gum in Church, which is the house of God.

Knowing all this, let us now enter the nave with a different mind, and let us participate fully in the Divine Liturgy.

Chapter Three

THE DIVINE LITURGY

At the end of *Orthros,* or Matins, we stand for the Doxology -- hymns giving praise and glory to God -- which brings us to the Divine Liturgy.

The Divine Liturgy is a constant dialogue; communication between the Priest and the faithful. It requires our full attention and participation, and it is strongly encouraged that we participate by chanting all or parts of the Liturgy.

To begin, the Priest raises the Holy Gospel and in a loud voice declares, "Blessed is the kingdom of the Father and the Son and the Holy Spirit, now and forever and to the ages of ages." At this moment, the Heavens open and we unite ourselves with the heavenly Kingdom. We bow our heads, making the sign of the cross.

During the Divine Liturgy there are certain times when we are allowed to sit. This is one of those times. We sit while the Priest or the Deacon recites the petitions. However, if a Bishop or Hierarch is present and celebrating the Divine Liturgy, we stand until the petition: "For our Archbishop…" is chanted. He will be standing at the

Despotikon, the Bishop's Throne. As the Choir chants, "*Eis Polla Eti Despota*," which in English means, "May you have many years," he gives us a blessing. At this point, we bow our heads, accepting his blessing. Then, we sit as the Priest continues with the rest of the petitions.

Petitions are prayers for every one of us and for all people. Since these are prayers, many people cross themselves as each one is chanted. To every petition, we respond, "*Kyrie Eleison*" or "Lord have Mercy," because only through His mercy can we be saved. With these two or three words, we express our desire to be with God.

If we really pay attention, we will realize that the Priest prays for every one of us and for everything in this world. The first three petitions are about peace. The Priest prays for peace from above, asking God to give us peace in our hearts and bodies. Only through Him, the "Angel of Peace," can we achieve peace and calm in our hearts and with one another. We cannot have peace with others unless we have peace within ourselves.

The Priest also prays for peace of the whole world, as well as for that particular Church and all her members. Without peace for the world, there cannot be peace within the Church. Through peace in the world, the

Church can become again "One, Holy, Catholic, and Apostolic Church" as the Holy Creed states. We see how important peace is for us Christians in the fact that the Priest blesses us repeatedly with the words "Peace be to all."

During this time, the Priest also prays for the health of our Archbishop and all clergy and laity, for that particular community, for good weather, bountiful crops, peaceful times, for all those who travel, and for protection from sickness and any danger. Finally, he prays that we may commit ourselves to Christ through the intercessions of Panagia. At this point, we cross ourselves, as well as every time we hear the words "to the Father and the Son and the Holy Spirit."

Following this portion of the Liturgy is the first *antiphon.* The Priest says, "Remembering our most holy, pure, blessed, and glorious Lady the Theotokos," and we cross ourselves. Here, we are asking the Mother of God to intercede for us. According to our beliefs, Panagia cannot save us -- only God saves us -- but she can ask her Son to have mercy on us and save us.

The word *antiphon* comes from the Greek words, "anti," which means opposite, and "*phoni*," which means voice. These hymns are called *antiphons* because at one time (and as is still the case in Greece) every Church had two cantors. One cantor was on the right side of the Church, next to the Bishop's throne, and the other was on the left. The first hymn was chanted by the first cantor on the right side and the second, by the cantor on the left, as if to be in response to one another.

The second *antiphon*, reminds us of Christ's birth, passion and Resurrection. The Priest says, "Save us, oh Son of God -- You God, who accepted incarnation, crucifixion, death and Resurrection, we pray to you, save us." We cross ourselves again, and every time we make reference to the Theotokos, Christ, the Holy Trinity, or any Saint's name.

For the third *antiphon*, we stand. At this point we sing one of the eight different hymns of the Resurrection. This happens for eight consecutive Sundays, at the end of which they start again from the beginning. (The eight hymns are listed at the end of this book.) On the major feast days we sing the hymn of that particular feast. For example, when we celebrate the Feast of Pentecost, we sing the hymn of Pentecost.

The third *antiphonon* is followed by the Small Entrance. At this time and every time the Priest is facing the congregation or is outside the Sanctuary, every movement by anyone has to stop. The faithful should not enter or leave the Nave. The Priest's presence in the Nave indicates that something important is taking place and, therefore, we should not disturb or interrupt what is going on.

THE SMALL OR LITTLE ENTRANCE

The Small or Little Entrance symbolizes the beginning of Christ's ministry, when he started teaching and preaching to the crowds. The Priest comes out holding the Gospel, the Word of God, accompanied by the Altar boys who are holding candles. The Gospel is Christ, and the candles, His light. The Priest blesses the Gospel and declares "*Sophia, Orthi*" or "Wisdom, Let us arise." The word "wisdom" refers to the Gospel, which is Christ, the true wisdom. The word "arise" is directed to the people; we should raise our minds and pray because the Gospel, Christ Himself, is in front of us, among us, coming to teach us, and, with His Angels, He is entering the Holy Altar. Therefore, we bow down our heads in reverence and in humility making the sign of the cross. The Priest enters the Holy Altar and places the gospel on the Holy Table.

We hear again the same hymn that preceded the Small Entrance, followed by the hymn of the day (the saint or the Feast we celebrate), and the hymn of the Patron Saint of that particular Church.

When we hear the *Trisagion* hymn, "*Agios o Theos*," or "Holy God," we cross ourselves, just as Prophet Isaiah did, (6:1-4) who heard the Angels constantly singing this hymn around God's throne. The hymn refers to the Holy Trinity -- the Father, the Son, and the Holy Spirit. With it, our voices here on earth join the voices of the Angels in heaven, and in one prayer, we glorify God. Let your mind imagine and visualize the moment. On major feast days, we chant two other hymns instead of the *Trisagion* hymn. The first begins with the words, "As many as have been baptized into Christ." This hymn is chanted on Epiphany, on the feast of St. John the Baptist, on the Saturday of Lazarus, on Holy Saturday morning, on Easter, during Bright Week, (the week after Easter), on Pentecost Sunday, on Monday - the feast of the Holy Spirit, and on Christmas Day. The second hymn, "We venerate your Cross and glorify your Resurrection," is chanted on the Feast of the Holy Cross on September 14th , and the third Sunday of the Great Lent.

After this, we sit to hear the Epistle reading.

THE EPISTLE READING

The Epistle readings are taken from the writings of the Apostles. They consist of letters that the apostles -- mainly Apostle Paul -- wrote to the people. Apostle Paul made three long trips. He visited many places in Greece and other places in the known world with the purpose of teaching the Christian faith and to Baptize people in the name of the Holy Trinity. After his trips, he sent the people letters to instruct them as to how to live a Christian life.

As soon as the Epistle reading is finished, we stand for the Gospel reading.

THE GOSPEL READING

The Gospel reading consists of a passage taken from the writings of the four Evangelists: Matthew, Mark, John, and Luke. These four Apostles wrote about the teachings and the events of Jesus' life the way they heard it, saw it, and witnessed it, and with the Grace and enlightenment of the Holy Spirit.

Can you imagine yourself among the crowds listening to Christ teaching two thousand-plus years ago? Can you imagine

Christ standing in front of you, talking to you? Well, He is. You are hearing Him speak as He spoke to His disciples and to the crowds. So, how do we respond? We bow down to the King, and we open our hearts and minds so we can accept His word, and make it a practice in our everyday lives.

And, how can we get the maximum benefit from this reading? First, we must be present physically and mentally. We must make every effort to come to Church on time. How can we approach the Holy Cup if we are not present to hear God's word? Also, we should not let our minds wander. We must open our ears to hear His word, and open our hearts to let His words dwell in us so that we can practice what we hear. In other words, we should fully and actively participate, both in body and in spirit.

At the end of the reading, we cross ourselves and prepare for the Great Entrance while we hear the Cherubic Hymn. This Hymn is directed toward the people; it instructs us how to behave. It invites us to prepare ourselves to accept Christ free of our worldly concerns and walk with Him though His passion. It is sung slowly so the Priest has time to offer incense to the Holy Table, the Icons on the *Iconostasis*, the faithful, and again, the Holy Table. The incense helps to uplift us spiritually. When the Priest incenses the faithful, it is not necessary to cross ourselves; we can just bow down our heads in reverence. After the incense, the Priest kisses the Holy Table and bows to the congregation. We bow our heads in response. Then, he proceeds towards the *Prothesis*, where he has prepared the Holy Gifts. Again, at this point, no one should be allowed to move around or enter the Nave.

THE GREAT ENTRANCE

During the Great Entrance, the Priest, along with the Altar boys who are carrying candles, the *Exapteriga,* and the censer, comes out of the Altar. In his left hand, he carries the Disk or Paten; in the right hand, the Chalice. As we mentioned earlier, there are pieces of bread on the Disk, each with its own meaning, that the Priest has cut out from the seal of the *Prosphoron*. The Chalice contains wine. On the Priest's back is a cloth that is tied around his neck. It is called the *Aera* or Aer. (See *The Holy Altar*.)

The Great Entrance represents the reason Christ came to the world: to bear His Cross, to die for each and every one of us, so that we can all be saved. It is Christ himself who is carrying His Cross to Golgotha. At this point in the Liturgy, we are to relive, in a way, His passion and Crucifixion. How do we respond to what is before us? We quietly bow, crossing ourselves, and we pray as we hear the Priest repeating these words, that He will "remember us unto His Kingdom," as He told the thief next to Him on the Cross.

The Priest enters the altar and places the Disk and Chalice on the Holy Table, covering both with the *Aer*, symbolically closing the tomb and rolling the stone over it. Then, he censes the gifts. The gifts are now ready to be sanctified. We may sit now, as the petitions begin, asking God to protect us and help guide us to live like Christ every day of our lives. The last six petitions refer to our spiritual life, asking God to grant us forgiveness, and offer us a peaceful and Christian end to our life on this earth. We cross ourselves in prayer to every petition that touches our hearts and minds. How wise is the Church to have in mind of all our needs and constantly pray for us?

The celebrant then declares, "Let us love one another..." In the past, it was customary at this point for the faithful to exchange the kiss of peace, essentially asking one another for forgiveness. Today, we do not usually do this, though some Churches still practice it. However, we still mentally pray and forgive those who have wronged us. If more than one celebrant Priest is present, they exchange the kiss of peace amongst each other. At the end of these petitions, the Priest blesses us, and we bow our heads. While some people make the sign of the cross, it is more common and more appropriate to do so when the Priest uses the Cross to bless the faithful. However, one should cross him or her self as he or she pleases.

Now the Priest leads us to confess our faith with the Holy Creed, declaring "The doors, the doors..." This is said because at this point during the early years of Christianity, the catechumen (those who were learning the faith but were not yet baptized as Christians, and who, as mentioned above, stood in the Narthex), and others that were not allowed in the Church, were supposed to leave. The doors were closed, allowing only the faithful to remain.

THE CREED

As the Creed is recited, the Priest takes the Aer in both hands and holding it as a drape, slowly shakes it over the gifts. As mentioned before, this symbolizes the earthquake that rolled away the stone and opened Christ's tomb.

The Creed is the dogma and basis of our Orthodox faith. We should all recite this prayer, crossing ourselves especially at the words "and in the Holy Spirit" and "in one, Holy, Catholic, and Apostolic Church…" Here, we do not pray specifically for the Catholic or Western Church, but for One Church in the World, one faith in Christ. The Greek word *"Katholiki"* means one faith in the whole world. We pray that one day we will all be united as one Church, the way it was before the western Church, the Catholic Church, was split from the true Orthodox Church of Christ.

ANAPHORA

After the Creed is recited, the *Anaphora* -- the preparation of the Divine Eucharist -- begins. It starts with the words, "Let us stand well. Let us stand in awe. Let us be attentive that we may present the holy offering in peace." Here the Priest tries to make the congregation aware by asking us to pay attention to what it will follow.

Now, a dialogue takes place between the Priest and the people, during which the people respond, "Mercy of peace, a sacrifice of praise" and the Priest responds, "The Grace of our Lord Jesus Christ and the love of God the Father and the communion of the

Holy Spirit be with you all." This Blessing is called Apostolic because it is the same blessing that Apostle Paul gave to the Corinthians. The Priest uses the Cross to bless us; therefore we should bow down and cross ourselves in prayer. The faithful answer "and with your spirit." The Priest raises his hands up and asks us to join him in lifting up our hearts. We respond "We lift them up to the Lord," thus opening our hearts and minds to accept Him free of any worldly thought. "Let us give thanks to the Lord," says the Priest, and we respond, "It is proper and right." This is the last response in this dialogue. The Priest now reads in low voice the Great Eucharistic prayer.

THE GREAT EUCHARISTIC PRAYER

While the Priest reads the Great Eucharistic prayer, we should all read along silently so we can understand its meaning. It is a prayer thanking God for all the blessings He has given us; through Him we are saved, renewed, resurrected from every sin. Then, aloud, the Priest tells us that the Angels around God's throne are praying -- "singing, voicing, proclaiming, and saying the triumphant hymn." The choir or the cantor continues the prayer with the "*Agios, Agios Agios, Kyrios*" ("Holy, Holy, Holy,

Lord Sabaoth"), the same hymn the crowds sang when Christ triumphantly entered Jerusalem, coming to his Passion. Likewise, we are now about to witness the great Sacrifice of Christ on the Altar Table as the preparation for the Sanctification of the Holy Gifts will take place.

At this point, the Priest reenacts the Last Supper, where Christ gave bread and wine to His disciples, by partaking in the bread and the wine and reciting the same words as Christ did: "Take, eat, this my Body, which is broken for the forgiveness of sins," and "Drink of it all; this my Blood of the new Covenant which is shed for you and for many for the forgiveness of sins." Christ instructed his disciples to do this in remembrance of Him. This is the oldest, the Holiest, and most important moment of the Divine Liturgy -- the moment that the bread and the wine are sanctified and changed, transformed into the Body and Blood of Christ. It is Christ Himself who, nailed on the Cross, is dying so that we can be resurrected and saved. It is He who changes the gifts into His own Body and His own Blood.

We solemnly kneel and prayerfully direct our thoughts to the Lord. Imagine yourself being there in front of the Cross, living and witnessing the Great Sacrifice. Feel His presence and the promise of the Eternal Life. Everything we are or have -- be it good health, family, jobs, or abundant earthly riches -- are gifts from above, granted to us by His Divine Grace. So, let us thank God with all our might during this very sacred time. The Priest offers our gifts on our behalf, as Christ offered Himself on the Cross for us. "We offer to You these gifts from Your own gifts in all and for all," the Priest says; in others words, we offer You, God, the gifts that you gave us, your gifts to you, for without you we would be nothing. The choir and the people respond "We praise You, we bless You, we give thanks to You and pray to You, Lord, our God."

If we open our hearts to God, we will feel His presence, His unending love, and His forgiveness. Let our hearts taste the gladness of Resurrection, and let us rejoice in our salvation.

We stand crossing ourselves as the Priest calls out, "And grant that in one voice and one heart we may glorify and praise Your most honored and majestic name, of the Father and the Son and the Holy Spirit, now and forever and to the ages of ages." Then, he blesses us, wishing all God's mercy to be on us. Crossing ourselves, we bow down in response, so that the mercy of God be upon the Priest as well. A few petitions follow, in which the Priest prays that we may be worthy not only to receive Christ through Holy Communion, but, after receiving Him, to be worthy and able to change our lives and become better people. At the end of these petitions, the Priest leads into the Lord's Prayer, which we should all recite together. Then, he blesses us one more time, and we respond by bowing down, accepting his blessing.

THE HOLY COMMUNION

Holy Communion is offered to all of us. However, only those who are baptized or chrismated into the Orthodox Church and are in full communion with the Church should partake of the Holy Gifts. Raising the Blessed Gifts with his hands, the Priest pronounces, "The Holy Gifts for the Holy people of God." What does this mean? Exactly what it says: the Holy gifts for the Holy people. Who are the Holy people, those worthy to receive the Holy gifts? We are. One might ask, who can be ready or worthy to receive Holy Communion every Sunday? Maybe none of us are. But, do we become more worthy by staying away, or waiting to be ready to receive Him? When will we be perfectly ready? Maybe never. As individuals with free will, with so many temptations in our lives, we might never be worthy to receive Him if we do not receive strength from Him. That is why we have confession. It is through confession and repentance that we ready ourselves.

All of us should see our Father confessor regularly. As we should continuously strive to become better people, we should not forget that we are human and, therefore, not perfect. Only God is perfect and without sin. Through confession, though, we come closer to perfection. Acknowledging and admitting our sins is the first step and leads to repentance. Christ told his disciples, and through them our Priests, that if they (the Priests) forgive our sins, they will be forgiven. Christ, therefore, commands us to seek the sacrament of Confession so that, cleansed from our sins, we can approach the Holy Cup and receive the Holy Eucharist.

Through Confession, we are strengthened. We become holier. We come to understand that it is God himself that dwells in us, and He and only He will enable us and direct us to become better people and to receive Him. It is through Him that we will find peace in our hearts and minds and, through this peace, we can love and forgive others.

It is a great sin to approach the Holy Cup unprepared. Communion is God Himself and we should make every effort to understand that. Therefore, having confessed our sins, let us approach the Holy Cup understanding our limitations, praying that God will strengthen us and guide us to become better individuals.

When the Priests says, "The Holy gifts for the Holy people of God," we should cross ourselves and respond with, "One is Holy, one is Lord, Jesus Christ, to the glory of God, the Father. Amen." This hymn encourages us to receive Communion, reminding us that only God is Holy. We are not perfect, but we should strive to become "God-like."

The Priest receives Holy Communion first, but before he does so, he turns to the people and asks their forgiveness. As mentioned above, the Priest is the one who forgives our sins through the sacrament of Holy Confession. We should bow down, showing him that we do forgive him. If we do not forgive him, how will we be able to approach the Holy Eucharist?

First, the Priest breaks the "Lamb," or *Amnos* (body), into four pieces, and places them on the Disk in the shape of a Cross. With this, we are reminded of the bruised body of Christ on the Cross. Then he takes the piece marked "IC" (*Isous Christos* which means "Jesus Christ") and, making the sign of the cross over the Chalice, he places the piece into the Chalice, thus uniting the Lord's soul with His body. He blesses the *Zeon* filled with boiling water, which symbolizes the warm faith with which we should approach the Holy Eucharist. After that, he reads specific prayers for Communion and he partakes of the Body of Christ. He drinks the Blood of Christ from the Cup, and then he prepares the gifts for us. In the Cup, he puts the remaining pieces or crumbs of the transformed bread, which is now the Body of Christ. Turning to the people, he invites us forward, saying, "With the fear of God, with faith and with love, draw near."

Let us examine these words closely. What kind of fear are we referring to? We do not fear that we might get sick from receiving Holy Communion. There are some people who try to go up first so that they won't get other people's germs. If we really understand the mystery of the Holy Sacrifice, and we believe that we are receiving our God and Savior, we should not fear sickness. Every Priest must consume what is left in the Holy Cup at the end of every Liturgy. If the Cup were a source of communicable diseases, all Priests would contract them. Therefore, we should not fear that we might catch something. We come with "fear" because fear is to be in awe and prayer, for we are about to receive Him in our bodies and hearts. We come with "faith" because we must believe that we are receiving Him, God Almighty. We come with "love" because we must have love for Him and for one another. Those receiving the Holy Gifts should approach with total humility in constant prayer. Make your cross, take the cloth with your hand and place it under your mouth, say your name to the Priest so that he can recite a prayer for you, and receive Holy Communion. Wipe your mouth, give the cloth to the next person, cross yourself, take the *antidoron* (blessed pieces of Bread), and go back to your pew, thanking God in prayer. When all who have come forward for Communion have partaken, the Priest raises the Chalice and says, "Save oh God your people and bless Your inheritance." At this point we cross ourselves and respond joyfully with the hymn beginning with, "We have seen the true light…," the light being the Resurrected Christ.

After offering incense to the Chalice, the Priest takes it in his right hand and takes the Paten or Disk in the left saying the words "blessed is our God." Turning to the faithful, he raises them up making the sign of the Cross, blessing us once more with the

Gifts as we bow our heads, crossing ourselves. He proceeds to the *Prothesis* where he places the disk and the Chalice. This symbolizes the Ascension of Christ. By this act, Christ is rejoining His Father in Heaven.

This takes us to the end of the Liturgy, as the Priest recites the dismissal prayer during which he invokes the saints to intercede for us. The choir, in return, responds by singing a prayer asking God to protect the Priest. Since he prays to God for us and on our behalf during the Liturgy, it is proper, in return, to pray for him.

After the Liturgy has concluded, the faithful come forward to receive the *Antidoron*, the blessed pieces of Bread. The word *Antidoron* comes from the words "anti," which means instead, and "*doron*," which means gift. All who did not receive the gift of Holy Communion receive the blessed bread as a gift, which reminds us that the Church thinks of everyone at all times.

While this bread is not the Body of Jesus, it has been blessed by the Priest on the Holy Table. Therefore, we must be careful not to drop it or allow pieces or crumbs to fall to the ground, where they might be stepped on. If you do not want to eat it right away, place it in a tissue and bring it home.

Chapter Four

Memorials And Fasting

Out of concern for our well-being, the Church has set some rules to help us in our liturgical and Christian lives. For the remainder of this book, I will provide information and rules for memorials, fasting, and other issues that concern all of us and will help us live an Orthodox Christian life.

Memorials

Commonly, we use the word "died" or "die" when people have departed from this life. The Church very wisely uses the words "sleep", or "falling asleep in the Lord". The word "die" refers to the separation of the body from the soul. The soul, freed from the body, lives in another world, different from the one we live in on earth. The details of where or how this world is, are unknown to us. We do know, however, that this world exists.

In various passages in the Bible, we get some idea of how the soul lives. Some examples include the parable of poor Lazarus (Luke 16:22) and the book of Revelation of St. John, which describe the

Second Coming of Christ and the Final Judgment.

We believe that on the Second Coming of Christ, He will judge us according to our life and actions on this earth. We, as people with free will, are capable of committing sins. Through confession, however, we can repent and get rid of our sins so that we can taste the Eternal Life.

Souls of the departed, after being separated from their bodies, live in a state according to their deeds. If a person has lived a Christ-like life here on earth, his or her soul will foretaste the joy of Paradise. If he or she has lived a sinful life and has not repented, even at the end, he or she will foretaste the fire and torture of hell.

Even though there are some sins that will not be forgiven in this life or the next (Matt. 12:31-33), it is our duty to pray for the souls of our beloved. Memorials are prayers conducted after or during the Divine Liturgy, asking the All Merciful God to show mercy to our beloved departed from this life. It is for this reason that we perform Memorials, or *Mnimosyna*.

For the memorials, we prepare the *Kollyva* by boiling wheat. The wheat symbolizes the souls and the new life that it is to come. Memorials may be performed any day of the year except on any Feast day of the Lord, any Feast day of the Theotokos, or during the period from the Saturday of Lazarus through the Sunday of Thomas (which is the Sunday after Easter).

We can also give the names of our deceased, as often as we can, to be read during the *Prothesis* (preparation of the Gifts) and at the Holy Table after the Consecration of the Gifts. Other things we can do include lighting candles in memory of those we have lost, or helping the poor and performing good deeds in their memory.

Fasting

Fasting, in general, is defined as the ability to control temptations, sins, and bad habits, as well as the abstention from certain foods. The Church has very wisely set certain periods of fasting, especially before major Holidays.

Fasting plays an important role in the life of every Christian, because, in a way, we cleanse our bodies and, at the same time, our souls. We are instructed how to fast in the Gospel reading of Cheese-Fare Sunday (last Sunday before Great Lent) (Matt. 6.16-18). "And when you fast, do not look dismal, like the hypocrites, for they disfigure their faces that their fasting may been seen by men. Truly I say to you, they have their reward.

But when you fast, anoint your head and wash your face, that your fasting may not be seen by men but by your Father who is in secret; and your Father who sees in secret will reward you." According to this, we should not boast about fasting, but fast in secret; the Father who sees what we do will reward us."

Fasting is dictated by the Church for our benefit; it is an exercise intended to make us mentally stronger. The Church recommends that we practice all the major Fasts - including some other days- throughout the year (you will find the fasts of the year listed later in this book). If we follow all these fast days, and we are spiritually and mentally ready, we can receive Holy Communion any time with a simple fast the day before and on that morning, assuming that we see our Father confessor regularly.

Below is what St. Chrysostom says about fasting.

Do you fast?
Give me proof of it by your works. If you see a poor man, take pity on him.
If you see a friend being honored, do not envy him.
Do not let [only] your mouth fast, but also the eye, and the ear and the feet and

the hands, and all the members of our bodies.
Let the hands fast, by being free of avarice. (Greed for wealth)
Let the feet fast by ceasing to run after sin.
Let the eyes fast by disciplining them to glare at that which is sinful.
Let the ear fast...by not listening to evil talk and gossip...
Let the mouth fast from foul words and unjust criticism.
For what good it is if we abstain from birds and fishes, but bite and devour our brothers?
Fast from discontent; feast on gratitude.
Fast from anger; feast on patience.
Fast from complaining; feast on appreciation.
Fast from unrelenting pressures; feast on unceasing prayer.
Fast from self-concern; feast on compassion for others.
Fast from discouragement; feast on hope.
Fast from lethargy; feast on enthusiasm.
Fast from suspicion; feast on trust.
Fast from gossip; feast on purposeful silence
Fast form words that pollute; feast on phrases that purify.

Fast from the seeming darkness; feast on the realities of Light.
Fast from hate and resentment; feast on love and good will.
Fast from thoughts that weaken; feast on promises that inspire.
Fast from problems that overwhelm; feast on prayer...

As I mentioned earlier, the peace of Christ in our hearts is very important for every Christian. In order to have peace, we must have love in our hearts. Through love, we forgive others and thus bring peace within us.

Peace and love go together with fasting. Fasting from foods is much easier than fasting from sinful acts. We can fast all we want from foods but, without love for one another, we cannot fast from our limitations.

To love is to forgive; to love is to see good things in your brother or sister; to love is to be positive, not to point out the negative in others. Helpful reading is the Epistle of St. Paul to the Romans (Chapter 12;9-21, Chapters 13 and 14;1-23). As St. Paul writes in his letter to the 1st Corinthians (Chapter 13;1-8):

If I speak in the tongues of men and angels but have not love, I am a noisy gong or a clanging cymbal. And if I have prophetic powers, and understand all mysteries and all knowledge, and if I have all faith, so as to remove mountains, but have not love, I am nothing. If I give away all I have, and if I deliver my body to be burned, but have not love I gain nothing. Love is patient and kind; love is not jealous or boastful; it is not arrogant of rude. Love does not insist on its own way; it is not irritable or resentful; it does not rejoice at wrong but rejoices in the right. Love bears all things, believes all things, hopes all things, endures all things. Love never ends.

Reading this passage, we can understand the power of love. I suggest we read this again and again until we fully comprehend it.

Love is the reason God sent his Son for us and for our salvation. Love is the reason that God will forgive us through the sacrament of confession. Through this love, we forgive others. Through this love, we accept one another. Through this love, we accept our limitations and faults and try to correct them. Through this love, we bring peace in our hearts. It is this love that will make us better human beings. It is this love that will bring us closer to one another. It is this love that will bring us closer to God and closer to Holy Communion.

The Greek Orthodox Archdiocese of America has published certain guidelines concerning the Sacramental life of its members. Listed below are the ones referring to Memorials, Fasting, Weddings, Divorce, Baptisms and Funerals as they appear in the ***Greek Orthodox Archdiocese Yearbook*** in simplified language.

MEMORIALS

The Church recommends that memorials for our loved ones should be performed as follows:

1. The third day after their death
2. The ninth day
3. The fortieth day (*Saranta*)
4. The anniversary of the first year
5. The anniversary of the third year

Memorials can also be conducted on the three Saturdays of Souls (*Psychosavata*), during the Great Lent and on the Pentecost Saturday of Souls.

Fasting

The fasting periods designated by the Church are:

1. All Wednesdays and Fridays of the year except those mentioned below.
2. January 5th, the day before the Epiphany of our Lord.
3. The last week before the Great Lent. It is called Cheese-fare week because only cheese and milk products, but no meat, are allowed.
4. The Great Lent, which starts with Clean Monday and ends the Saturday of Lazarus.
5. Holy Week, including Holy Saturday, which is a day of strict fast including abstention from oil.
6. The Fast of the Apostles. This fast can be very short or long, depending of when Easter falls. It starts the Monday after the Feast of All Saints and ends on June 28th.
7. The Fast of the Dormition of Panagia. It starts August 1st and ends on the 15th, with the exception of August 6th -- the Transfiguration of the Lord -- on which fish is allowed.
8. On August 29th, the Feast of the Beheading of St. John the Baptist.

9. On September 14, the Exaltation of the Holy Cross.
10. The Christmas Lent of Nativity of the Lord, from November 15 to December 24. During the Christmas fast, we are allowed to consume fish, wine and oil, except on Wednesdays and Fridays.

Below are fast days on which fish, wine, and oil are allowed, even though they fall during Fast periods.

1. On March 25th , the feast of the Annunciation.
2. On Palm Sunday.
3. On August 6th, as mentioned above
4. On November 21st, the Feast of the Entrance of Panagia to the Temple.

Days that are fast free (includes Wednesdays and Fridays):

1. The first week of the *Triodion*, which starts on the Sunday of the Publican and Pharisee, and ends on the Sunday of the Prodigal Son.
2. The Bright Week, which is the week after Easter.
3. The week after Pentecost
4. From Christmas, December 25th to January 4$^{th.}$

Chapter Five

WEDDINGS AND MARRIAGE

WEDDINGS

In order for a man and a woman to be married in the Orthodox Church, they must adhere to the following procedures:

1) The Wedding must be celebrated by an Orthodox Priest in an Orthodox Church with the permission of the diocesan Bishop. Both the Priest and the Church must belong to a canonical Orthodox jurisdiction. In other words, a Catholic or Protestant Priest cannot perform a wedding in an Orthodox Church, and an Orthodox Priest cannot perform a wedding in a Catholic or Protestant Church.

2) For the Bishop's permission, the Priest must make sure of the following:
   a) The persons getting married have not been married before.
   b) The persons getting married are not related to each other.

c) If one or both are widowed, they must present the death certificate(s) of the deceased spouse(s).
d) If one or both have been previously married in the Orthodox Church, they must have obtained ecclesiastical as well as civil divorce(s).
e) If one or both are members of a parish, but their marriage is to be performed in a different parish, they must provide a certificate verifying that they are members in good standing with their parish for the current year.
f) The couple must present the Priest with a civil marriage license.

3) No person may marry more than three times in the Church; a third marriage can only be performed with special permission from the Bishop.

4) Marriage between an Orthodox and non-Orthodox Christian is permitted only if the non-Orthodox has been baptized, in water, in the Name of the Father and the Son and the Holy Spirit. An Orthodox Christian cannot be married to a non-Christian.

5) The Sponsor (*Koumbaros* or *Koumbara*) must be an Orthodox Christian in good standing with the Church. If the Sponsor is married, his marriage must have been blessed in the Orthodox Church. If he is divorced, he must have an ecclesiastical divorce; otherwise he cannot be a sponsor. Non-Orthodox persons may be members of the wedding party only.

6) Marriages are not allowed on the following days: during the Great Lent and Holy Week and Easter; Holy Pentecost; August 1-15; August 29 (Beheading of St. John the Baptist); September 14 (Exaltation of the Holy Cross); December 13-25; Epiphany (January 5 and 6). Marriages may be performed on these days only by permission of the diocesan Bishop.

INTER-CHRISTIAN MARRIAGES

The Orthodox Church will bless marriages between Orthodox and non-Orthodox only when:

1. The non-Orthodox is a Christian who has been baptized, in water, in the

Name of the Father and the Son and the Holy Spirit; and

2. If the couple accept to baptize their children in the Orthodox Church and raise them according to the Orthodox Faith and Tradition.

If an Orthodox Christian has been married in a non-Orthodox Church, he or she is no longer in good standing with the Church, and is not allowed to receive the Sacraments of the Church, including Holy Communion, or become a Sponsor of an Orthodox Marriage, Baptism or Chrismation.

The non-Orthodox husband or wife of a married Orthodox Christian, whose marriage has been blessed in the Orthodox Church, is not allowed to receive the Sacraments, including Holy Communion, be buried by the Church, serve as Sponsor, serve on the Parish Council, or vote in parish assemblies or elections.

In order for a non-Orthodox person to fully participate in the Life of the Church, he or she must be either Chrismated (if that person is a Christian) or, if he or she is a non-Christian, be Baptized in water in the name of the Holy Trinity, given that he or she learns the faith through the Priest. If someone chooses not to follow these rules, then he or she will not be able to fully participate in the sacramental life of the Church.

PROHIBITED MARRIAGES

Marriage is not allowed between the following:

1. Parents with their own children, grandchildren or great-grandchildren, or godchildren of the same godparents.
2. Brothers-in-law and sisters-in-law.
3. Uncles and aunts with nieces and nephews.
4. First cousins with each other.
5. Foster parents with foster children or foster children with the children of foster parents.
6. Godparents with godchildren or godparents with the parents of their godchildren.

DIVORCE

The parish Priest must exhaust every effort to reconcile a couple that is considering divorce. If the Priest fails to reconcile the couple, and they have been issued a civil divorce, the Priest will submit a petition accompanied by the civil divorce, seeking the ecclesiastical divorce, to the Spiritual Court of the Diocese.

The person(s) seeking the divorce must be a member in good standing with the parish. Orthodox Christians of the Greek Orthodox Archdiocese who have been granted a civil divorce but not an ecclesiastical divorce may not participate in any sacraments of the Church, or serve on the Parish Council, until they have been granted a divorce by the Church.

Chapter Six

BAPTISMS AND FUNERALS

BAPTISMS

A person who wishes to become a sponsor for Baptism or Chrismation must be an Orthodox Christian in good standing and a supporting member of an Orthodox parish. A person may not serve as a Godparent if his or her marriage has not been blessed by the Church, if he or she is civilly divorced but has not been granted an ecclesiastical divorce, or if he or she is not in communion with the Orthodox Church for any other reason.

Baptisms may not be performed from Christmas Day through the Feast of Theophany (December 25-January 6), during Holy Week, or on any of the Great Feast Days of the Lord.

FUNERALS

Funeral services are permitted on any day of the year, except for Sundays and Holy Friday, unless permission is granted from the area Bishop.

Chapter Seven

Antiphons - Hymns of the Resurrection

First Tone

Though the tomb was sealed by a stone and soldiers guarded Your pure body, You arose, O Savior, on the third day, giving life to the world. Therefore, O Giver of life, the heavenly powers praise You: Glory to Your resurrection, O Christ, glory to Your kingdom, glory to Your plan of redemption, O only loving God.

Second Tone

When you descended unto death, O life immortal, You destroyed Hades with the splendor of Your divinity. And when You raised the dead from the depths of darkness, all the heavenly powers shouted: O Giver of life, Christ our God, glory to You.

Third Tone
Let the heavens rejoice and earth be glad, for the Lord has shown the power of His reign: He has conquered death by death, and become the first born of the dead. He has delivered us from the depths of Hades; and has granted to the world great mercy.

Fourth Tone
The joyful news of Your resurrection was told to the women disciples of the Lord by the angel. Having thrown off the ancestral curse, and boasting, they told the Apostles: death has been vanquished, Christ our God is risen, granting to the world great mercy.

Fifth Tone
To the Word, coeternal with the Father and the Spirit, born of the Virgin for our salvation, let us, the faithful, give praise and worship. Of His own will He mounted the cross in the flesh, He suffered death, and raised the dead by His glorious resurrection.

Sixth Tone
The heavenly powers appeared at Your tomb, and those guarding it became like dead. Mary stood at Your grave seeking

Your pure body. You stripped the power of hades, not touched by its corruption. You met the virgin woman, as one who grants life. O Lord, who rose from the dead, glory to You.

Seventh Tone

By Your cross You destroyed death, and to the thief You opened paradise. You transformed the sorrow of the Myrrhbearers, and commanded the Apostles to proclaim that You have risen from the dead, Christ our God, granting to the world great mercy.

Eighth Tone

From on high You descended, O merciful Lord, and accepted the three-day burial to free us from our passions. Glory to You, O Lord, our life and our resurrection.

ΑΝΑΣΤΑΣΙΜΑ – ΑΠΟΛΥΤΙΚΙΑ

Ηχος α΄

Του λίθου σφραγισθέντος υπό των Ιουδαίων, και στρατιωτών φυλασσόντων το άχραντον σου σώμα, ανέστης τριήμερος Σωτήρ, δωρούμενος τω κοσμώ την ζωήν. Δια τούτο αι δυνάμεις των ουρανών εβόων σοι ζωοδότα. Δόξα τη αναστάσει σου Χριστέ, δόξα τη βασιλεία σου, δόξα τη οικονομία σου, μόνε φιλάνθρωπε.

Ηχος β΄

Ότε κατήλθες προς τον θάνατον, η ζωή η αθάνατος, τότε τον άδην ενέκρωσας, τη αστραπή της θεότητος, ότε δε και τους τεθνεώτας, εκ των καταχθόνιων ανέστησας, πάσαι αι δυνάμεις των επουρανίων εκραύγαζον Ζωοδότα Χριστέ, ο Θεός ημών, δόξα σοι.

Ηχος γ΄

Ευφραινέσθω τα ουράνια, αγαλλιάσθω τα επίγεια, ότι εποίησε κράτος, εν βραχίονι αυτού, ο Κύριος, επάτησε τω θανάτω τον θάνατον πρωτότοκος των νεκρών εγένετο, εκ κοιλίας άδου ερρύσατο ημάς, και παρέσχε τω κόσμω το μέγα έλεος.

Antiphons - Hymns of the Resurrection

Ηχος δ΄

Το φαιδρόν της αναστάσεως κήρυγμα, εκ του αγγέλου μαθούσαι αι του Κυρίου μαθήτριαι, και την προγονικήν απόφασιν απορρίψασαι, τοις αποστόλοις καυχώμεναι έλεγον, εσκύλευται ο θάνατος, ηγέρθη Χριστός ο Θεός, δωρούμενος τω κόσμω το μέγα έλεος.

Ηχος πλ. α΄

Τον συνάναρχον Λόγον Πατρί και Πνεύματι, τον εκ παρθένου τεχθέντα εις σωτηρίαν ημών, ανυμνήσωμεν πιστοί και προσκυνήσωμεν ότι ηυδόκησε σαρκί, ανελθείν εν τω Σταυρώ, και θάνατον υπομείναι, και εγείραι τους τεθνεώτας, εν τη ενδόξω αναστάσει αυτού.

Ηχος πλ. β΄

Αγγελικαί δυνάμεις επί το μνήμα σου, και οι φυλάσσοντες, απενεκρώθησαν και ίστατο Μαρία εν τω τάφω, ζητούσα το άχραντον σου σώμα. Εσκύλευσας τον άδην, μη πειρασθείς υπ' αυτού, υπήντησας τη παρθένω, δωρούμενος την ζωήν. Ό αναστάς εκ των νεκρών, Κύριε δόξα σοι.

Ηχος βαρύς

Κατέλυσας τω Σταυρώ σου τον θάνατον ηνέωξας τω ληστή τον παράδεισον, των μυροφόρων τον θρήνον μετέβαλες, και τοις σοις αποστόλοις κηρύττειν επέταξας, ότι ανέστης Χριστέ ο Θεός, παρέχων τω κόσμω το μέγα έλεος.

Ηχος πλ. δ΄

Εξ ύψους κατήλθες ο εύσπλαγχνος, ταφήν κατεδέξω τριήμερον, ίνα ημάς ελευθέρωσης των παθών. Η ζωή και η ανάστασις ημών, Κύριε δόξα σοι.

Chapter Eight

RECIPES

PROSPHORON

Prosphoron is the bread that the Priest uses for the Divine Liturgy. The word, *Prosphoron* comes from the Greek word *prosphero* or *prosphora* which means, offering. The faithful prepare the bread at home and take it to the Church accompanied with a list of names that they wish to have commemorated, either for the health of the living or in memory of our deceased, or both. Make sure you mark the list so the Priest can read the names appropriately. Before you start with making the prosphoro, you should pray, and meditate. This, after all, will be transformed into the body of Christ. The preparation of the Holy Gifts is taking place in the Orthros (Matins) service, so make sure you take it to Church very early on Sunday morning or the day before. Many thanks to the Ladies of Philoptochos at the Holy Trinity Church in Bridgeport, CT who were kind to provide us with the recipes for Prosphoro, Artoklasia and Kollyva.

INGREDIENTS

6 -7 c. flour shifted all purpose, unbleached or bread flour
1 tsp. salt
2 ½ c warm water (too hot might prevent the yeast from rising- too cold might take very long time)
1 Tbsp. dry, active yeast.
1 tsp. sugar (optional)
1 round 10 inch pan
1 *Prosphoro* seal

In a large mixing bowl, mix water, salt, yeast, sugar (if using) and 4 cups flour. Beat at medium speed and continue adding flour one cup at a time, until the dough comes away from the bowl. Remove the dough to a floured surface and knead until it is soft and smooth. Form into a circle and place in a lightly floured 10 inch pan. Lightly flour the *Prosphoro* seal and press it on top and in the middle of the *Prosphoro*. Before removing the seal, with a toothpick, prick around the seal in the shape of a cross (once on top, once at bottom and once on each side). Gently remove the seal. Prick around the edges of the imprint of the seal and at each inside corner of the seal. Place the bread in a warm place and let rise till doubled. Bake at 350 in a pre warmed oven for 40-45 minutes. (Bottom should be golden brown). Remove from oven and let it cool on a rack. Once it has cooled wrap in plastic and then in foil.

KOLLYVA (BOILED WHEAT)

As we have said, we prepare *Kollyva* for the memorials. We use wheat because from the seed we get life. The seed is planted in the dark soil, as Christ died and descended into Hades for us. The seed produces life and crops, as Christ was Resurrected from the dead, with the promise of life everlasting. The ingredients used, signify the sweetness of life (sugar) and the bitterness of death (cumin). When you are ready to assemble the *Kollyva*, light your *kantili* and pray for your diseased loved ones. You may divide this recipe for smaller tray or bowl.

Ingredients

For mixture:

3 lbs. Shelled wheat
12 oz cracker meal
8 oz. sugar
6 tsp. ground cinnamon (rounded)
2 tsp. cumin (rounded)
½ lb. golden raisins
1 lb. chopped walnuts
2 c sesame seeds (toasted)
1 large mixing bowl
1 large tray (approximately 18x12)

For topping

With the following ingredients, you will cover the exposed wheat completely. How much you will need depends on the size and shape of your plate and the moisture of the wheat. Have all your ingredients ready from the night before the assembly.

Powdered sugar as needed
White sugar coated almonds for decoration
Cracker meal, as needed
Browned flour as needed (you brown flour by baking it in the oven and stirring it from time to time until is lightly brown)
Six large White doilies
Wax paper
2 medium sieves (one of the cracker meal and flour and a clean one for the powdered sugar)

Friday night: Place the whole wheat in a large 8 quart stainless steal pot and fill it with cold water. Soak overnight covered.

Saturday morning: Drain the wheat into a large colander. Place the wheat in the rinsed out pot and refill with fresh water, ¾ from the top. Bring to boil. Lower the heat and simmer on low for 2 to 2 1/2 hours, stirring every few minutes to avoid sticking or burning on bottom of the pot. As water evaporates add more water to reach the original water line of ¾ full. Water will get cloudy and pasty. When wheat is soft to touch and taste, remove from heat. Pour off liquid into a colander so as not to lose any of the wheat. Rinse well with cold water. Repeat process several times until water remains clear and the wheat is not starchy. On a large countertop or table, spread a large towel and cover with lint free cloth. Spread the wheat to cover the whole cloth leaving 2 inch perimeter all around. Add the raisins and spread over wheat. Cover with another lint free cloth. Fold in edges. You can just leave it like this until the next morning. In the summer when the weather is hot, fold it in a bundle and place it in the refrigerator.

Sunday morning: Carefully place the wheat in a large mixing bowl. Add cracker meal, browned flour, sesame seeds, walnuts, cinnamon, and sugar and mix well.

Assembly:

Place six white paper doilies around the tray and place a square piece of wax paper in the center of the tray. With your hands take the wheat mixture and place it in the

tray making a cross. Continue in the same manner until all wheat is on the tray forming a mount in the center. Take a large piece of wax paper and place on top of the wheat, pressing firm and smooth. Remove the paper. Sift cracker meal all over so you cover the whole area. Place the wax paper in the same manor and press down again. Sift browned flour and repeat the same process with the wax paper. With a clean sieve, sift enough powdered sugar over the flour to cover the whole area. With a clean wax paper, repeat the process. Use more powdered sugar if needed in order to cover the flour completely. Brush excess sugar from around edges with a small brush. Add the candy almonds around the tray. Using the candy almonds form a cross in the middle of the tray and on the mount. In the same manner form the initial of the first name of the deceased on the left of the cross and the initial of the last name to the right of the cross. Take it carefully to the Church and place it on the designated table.
Don't forget to give the names of the deceased written on a piece of paper to the Priest.

ARTOKLASIA (BLESSING OF THE FIVE LOAVES)

Besides the *Prosphoron*, the faithful also offer *Artotklasia.* The word comes from the Greek words *Artos* (bread) and *klasia* which means “cut or break”. It consists of five round loaves of sweet bread. We offer them in remembrance of the miracle that Christ performed in the dessert feeding five thousand people from five loaves of bread. It is offered by the faithful for the health of their families, or in honor of a saint celebrating His or Her feast day. We take the five loaves to Church accompanied by the names of living family members, since it is offered for our health and well-being. The breads are placed on a table along with two small bottles, one filled with oil and the other with wine, the most essential elements of food- and five candles. At the appropriate time, the Priest will conduct a small service where he will bless the five loaves and he will commemorate the names of the people who offered these gifts and/or for whom they were offered. After the blessing of the loaves, the bread will be cut in pieces and distributed to the faithful present.

Ingredients
10 lbs. flour
1 lb. fresh yeast
1 lb. unsalted butter
22 eggs beaten
3 eggs beaten with 1 tsp. oil for glaze
4 c milk divided
8 c sugar
4 Tbsp. Crisco shortening
1 c. warm water
3 Tbsp. *mahlepi* (sold in Greek markets) or grated orange peel
5 12”- 14” round pans 2”- 4” deep

Warm 1c milk and mix it with 1c warm water 1 Tbsp. sugar and mix all with the yeast until it dissolves. Set it aside for 5-10 minutes, covered loosely with plastic wrap.

In a saucepan, melt butter with Crisco. Cool slightly. In another saucepan, melt sugar with milk until sugar dissolves. Cool slightly.

In a large mixing bowl mix flour, yeast mixture, butter, sugar mixture, beaten eggs and *mahlepi*. Mix well, and kneed for 15-20 minutes. Allow dough to rise covered with plastic wrap for 1-11/2 hrs. Divide into five pieces and kneed each one for 3-5 minutes more. Work into round loaves (should be 3-4 inches thick, flat and round). Place in a round greased pan, cover with plastic wrap and let rise in a warm place for about 2hrs.

Brush the glaze on each loaf making sure you cover the top and all exposed area well. Bake in a 350 pre heated oven for 35-40 minutes. Remove from the oven and let them cool in pans for 30 minutes. Remove from pans and cool completely. Wrap in plastic bags and take them to Church. This recipe may be cut in half for smaller loaves

EPILOGUE

I hope this book has helped you to better understand what is going on during the Divine Liturgy. As we have discussed, the Divine Liturgy is filled with great symbolism and spirituality, wisely put together for one purpose only: to unite us with our Creator through Holy Communion. We should constantly try to be as present as possible. Distractions are plenty -- people entering or moving around, children crying, thoughts of mundane matters. The best way to remain focused is to participate actively by following the Divine Liturgy book and chanting along with the choir or the cantor.

If we pay attention and allow ourselves to be totally attuned to all that is unfolding in front of our eyes, we can be uplifted and transformed, mentally and spiritually, and we can experience the mysticism of the Holy Eucharist.

Parents, and especially mothers, bear the primary responsibility of teaching their children the basic elements of the Divine Liturgy, and it is very important that they do so. Our job of fostering our children's spiritual life does not end with their baptism but, rather, requires constant instruction.

So, how do we fulfill this duty and sacred task? We can start by teaching them small things: how to cross themselves, how to behave in Church, some easy hymns, and the Lord's Prayer. As they grow older, we can add more hymns and more prayers. All the hymns and prayers that I know I learned from childhood.

We should start teaching children from a very early age. Bring your children to Church. If they are restless, take them out until they calm down, and then return with them for the service. In removing them for a moment, we show sensitivity and consideration to others who are also there to pray.

Once your children are baptized, take them up for Holy Communion every Sunday so that they learn and are not afraid of the Priest. Fasting is not necessary for small children or infants. A Bishop was once asked what fast was appropriate to practice for children. His recommendation was that up to age seven or eight, they can have a very light breakfast before Church. After that age they should fast as adults.

Above all, children learn by example. Therefore, we must be very careful how we behave in Church. If we do not show them how to actively participate in the Liturgy, they may never learn. We must attend

Church regularly. It is not enough to drop our children off for Sunday school and pick them up afterwards. What is more important than praying together as a family? Children do what they see us do.

Families that pray together, stay together. Be involved in your children's lives by praying with them, whether at home or in Church.

As you can see, I have included some guidelines for fasting, baptisms, days when marriages, funerals, and memorials are not allowed. Also included are recipes for *prosphoro* and kolyva, as well as other information that may be useful.

As I stated in the beginning, the reason I wrote this book was to inform and explain, in simple words, the Divine Liturgy to the common person. Please read it, study it with an open mind, and learn the basics of the Divine Liturgy, which is so rich in symbolism and spirituality.

It is my prayer that everyone who reads this book will benefit in some way and will be able to comprehend and participate fully in with greater understanding of the Divine Liturgy.

BIBLIOGRAPHY

Living The Liturgy by
Rev. Stanley S. Harakas Light and Life Publ. Co.

The Divine Liturgy, Rev. Nicholas M. Elias, 4th Edition, "Astir" Publishing

The Divine Liturgy and Sunday Gospels, Ecumenical Publishing

Holy Bible the New King James Version, Thomas Nelson Publishing

The New England Bible- New Testament, 2nd Edition, Oxford Publishing

H Theia Latreia, Apo ton Ourano sten Ye– the Holy Worship, from Heavens to Earth" Rev. George A. Kalpouzos. Photothotes publishing

Index

7310154R0

Made in the USA
Charleston, SC
16 February 2011